Mary Magdalene:
Revelations from a First Century Avatar
Volume III

Gloria Amendola

GRAVE DISTRACTIONS PUBLICATIONS
NASHVILLE, TN

Mary Magdalene:
Revelations from a First Century Avatar
Volume III

by: Gloria Amendola

Grave Distractions Publications
Nashville, Tennessee
www.gravedistractions.com

ISBN-13: 978-0-9908685-2-1
In Publication Data
Amendola, Gloria
Categories:
1.Mind, Body, and Spirit 2. Channeling & Mediumship
BISAC Code: OCC003000

Printed in the United States

Table of Contents

Introduction

It's only a matter of time before more evidence concerning our hidden history appears from the shadows. These fragments, when put together, will reveal a more accurate account of ETs, shadow governments, hidden agendas and the like. And these fragments will include some shocking revelations when it comes to the Jesus story—a story that undoubtedly involves Mary Magdalene.

⚜ ⚜ ⚜

Religion is fading away in the West. Many people are no longer interested in the dogma and social restrictions that religion demands of them. In this day and age, individuals are breaking free from obsolete ideas and biased thinking. With the Piscean Age ending and it's impetus of religious beliefs forced upon us, many of us are now choosing direct personal experience that is born from intuition, insight, and observance.

So it makes sense that many of us are interested in spirituality. We're curious about the nature of our reality and are asking bold questions in the process. We want to *know* ourselves more fully—and this is a knowing that comes from an ancient Gnostic wisdom buried deep inside our souls. We want to remember it, so we can live more authentic lives, and embrace our vast human potential. As we transition into the coming Aquarian Age, we're exploring many pathways of truth, and rediscovering our world through the eyes of the Ancient Ones.

⚜ ⚜ ⚜

In this volume you may feel that Magdalene has increased the intensity of her message. My sense is that the pull between the polarities of dualistic thinking is growing stronger day by day. Tension between opposing forces is increasing. That signals to me we are shifting even more. But what exactly are we shifting into? Is it a world we want to live in, or someplace else entirely? Is it a state of being that feels aligned to the incoming galactic light? Or is it a feeling that things are moving in the wrong direction? Will such extremes be the catalyst to crack open our world and let all creation flow? And if so, what exactly does that mean for us?

In Volume III of Magdalene's revelations, Mary is helping us reclaim what's been lost—the ancient wisdom teachings. She's providing further insight into mysteries that have eluded us for so long. Again, this tells me we are ready to receive these pearls of wisdom.

As you read the final sentiments in Mary's memoir, ask yourself— do her words move you to tears? Do they startle you or make perfect sense? What have Mary's teachings meant to you? Have you questioned your beliefs because of them? Do you see religion in different light? Have her words moved you deeper into your journey? Do you feel deceived by those in positions of power? And if so, *why* have you been deceived—for what purpose?

Well hang on to your hats because this last tome just might rock your world. It will shed a bright light on the nature of our reality. Mary says she's revealing these things now because there's no more time to waste. She says our most critical hour is upon us. It sounds scary at times, but despite the darkness flooding our world, Magdalene has great hope for humanity!

As the goddess often does, Mary is holding the mirror for us, up close and personal. Magdalene is asking that we begin to see our reflection without the distortion that's been part of our existence for thousands of years. As the mental programming is exposed in all its hideous forms, Mary reminds me that many will be left dazed and confused.

Thankfully Mary Magdalene is with us. She's providing instructions for clearing emotions and beliefs that keep us stuck in our wounding. Her words of wisdom are like a healing balm so desperately needed, although sometimes they can feel like the sting of a bee!

Mary Magdalene is also laying the groundwork for the Immortality Teachings, why they were so important to preserve, and why they must be revealed at this time. In Volume III, she answers many questions that are precursors to understanding those teachings.

The actual Immortality Teachings will come from Jesus himself. The Great Teacher will bring forth this eternal knowledge, but before he does, Magdalene must reveal The True Baptism. To prepare the Way, she'll teach us how to use this ancient technique to activate our genetic code.

These ancient wisdom teachings that Mary is revealing are needed more than ever. They can help us transition from material addiction to spiritual freedom. They can help us recognize all that's good for us, and for the earth. These teachings can provide further insights into the golden mean and Fibonacci spiral. They can serve to remind us that living things are mandated by this intelligent blueprint. And it's the honoring of that design that can bring us back into balance.

Thankfully Mary Magdalene is revealing what was once kept secret. She's teaching us to embrace the feminine wisdom once more. And from that understanding, Mary is guiding us with exceptional intelligence and love, and a truly forgiving heart.

My hope is that she can guide you too, at this time of the prophesied Shift of the Ages.

The Divine Duo: St. Baume, France

Chapter 1
Magdalene's Memoir Concludes

In this chapter, Mary Magdalene provides the final details of her extraordinary life.

My questions are in italics within her narrative. At times I needed clarification, and wanted to know more. And so the dialogue begins...

Mary Magdalene:

It was nearing the time when we would be traveling our separate ways. There were roads to trek and teachings to impart. We were masters of our time called upon by the Ancient Ones. And their directive for us was to further instruct our people of the Creator's blueprint inside of them.

We did not wish to separate from our family but we had agreed to this mission long before the children were born. In truth, we had agreed to this mission long before we ever took on physical form. Yet in my private moments when I walked down by the river, I would cry my own river of tears. I did not want to say goodbye to my children, to Great Mother Mary, and especially to my beloved. No, in those moments I felt as if our gifts were our curse! Our gifts called on us to give of ourselves that which we had mastered. And the price for that mastery was service to others, just like mother had always taught me.

There were times I held deep resentments inside of me. Yeshua knew when I felt this way and he would remind me that these feelings were not of my mastery. I knew that. Of course I knew that! But I wanted to spend my life with my family. Besides, had we not we sacrificed enough? Truly I was aware these thoughts were not of my mastery. They were born from my desire to lead a simple life and be with my family. And I do not apologize for such feelings, for this was my truth.

Yet we always knew the time would come when we would have to complete our Mission of Light. It involved merging our light bodies with the sacred places on the earth, for we were asked to seed new thought forms for the coming age. We actively engaged the Guardians to help us along the way, so there would be no interference by those who wished to thwart our mission here on earth.

When you say Guardians, do you mean the Guardians of the Grail?

Yes.

What was the grail back then?

The grail has been many things throughout time. But first and foremost, the grail is consciousness. It is an awareness of being that is not in your present scope of understanding.

Is it a certain kind of consciousness?

It is an immortality consciousness.

What does that mean?

The light body transfers mathematical codes into the molecular structure of a sentient being, for purposes of ascension. Immortality is the ultimate form of ascension.

How so?

In that process we take our memories with us. We allow the internal light to penetrate our deepest layers of being. We acknowledge our original instructions which come from the energy of the stars and beyond. Our external power source is celestial but our ascension is internal. It is the way we were designed.

Okay, let me see if I understand what you're saying to me.

Before you do that, let me add this piece. When we become like a star, we radiate the interstellar light. We move into the galactic corridor as filaments of the divine spark, as a reflection of that awareness. The Creator acknowledges that by lighting our spark with even more energy. You would know this as an atomic explosion. But that is an outer action. This is more of an implosion, an inner reaction. It helps our light bodies acquire more heat and reflection. This is part of the High Science that was so well understood in my beloved Egypt. The afterlife was known to carry great force, so one could influence earth from an expanded state.

Why do you want to carry your memories of earth with you?

That is part of the immortality process. Those memories are important because they carry great charge from the heart. Without that charge, we could not achieve immortality!

Is this how heart based intelligence works?

Yes. The density here can be quite difficult to cast off. However, the interaction with matter and spirit creates a focal point for the Creator's light, which can become more fully expressed in us in a way that benefits harmony and wholeness. And that focal point is in the field of the heart.

Okay, it's making a little more sense. So there's no going to the 5th dimension?

No. The 5th dimension is right in front of you. It always has been. But many of you are still not compatible with that dimension. You do not have access to it yet. Yet it is there, it exists. And when you are ready, you will vibrate there very quickly. But there is a catch.

What is it?

If you allow yourselves to return to dualistic thinking, you quickly move from one dimension to the other. It's a frequency, and sometimes moving about so quickly can hurt you.

How do we stop ourselves from doing that?

You must finally break free from your mental movies.

You mean we have to become aware of our mental programming?

Exactly! Those of us who spent time in the temples were taught by great teachers who reminded us that becoming the grail meant awakening to our immortality.

How did that help people break free from their programming?

We could take on exciting opportunities to experience the magic of ourselves. We could project our awareness from location to location, with much more energy and pulse. It was as if we were joining in on the Battle of the Titans. You see, there was great conflict raging here on earth. If you study the ancient stories, you will find there has been intervention here by other races since the beginning of time. The forces of light and darkness, in all their emanations, have fueled this clash.

Do you mean ETs?

Other forms of intelligence have fought over who would dominate as a species on earth.

Who won?

It is an ongoing battle, but with this new cycle of time, the light is searing itself into the earth body now. That penetrating force is with you in many ways.

Then why is there still so much corruption and pollution in modern times?

Think about that. If the earth is increasing the light in her body, would she not be exposing such corruption? Would she not be expelling that which has been so poisonous to her?

Yes.

Then remain confident this terrible corruption upon your lands will be exposed in due time. It will be reduced in its influence in the months and years to come.

With the recent data on climate change, it seems we don't have years to get this right.

Keep supporting those who support cleansing the environment; support those technologies that are coming forth now. One of the missions of the young ones is to formulate remedial solutions. Realize those solutions are a direct result of those of you who are seeding new thought forms into your world right now. That is *your* mission!

I've been part of these efforts for years—to restore the flow of meridian energies in and around the earth.

And do you see a change in your world as a result of your work?

Yes, but sometimes it gets frustrating.

The frustration comes from your expectations. Do you not get wonderful signs and miracles when you have done this work? Did the dragonflies not appear in great numbers when you cleared the lands that held memory of the Indian massacres in Massachusetts?

Yes they did. They were everywhere. But sometimes it feels like no one will ever acknowledge or respect the work of so many who have tirelessly traveled and worked with the global grid system of earth. We heard the calling to work in this way to heal our world. And yet very few are even aware of this grid.

It is a powerful technology you have mastered!

Still, I do feel your weariness. So let me take you back to our story, to what we had to do to complete our greater mission in the world of our time. And please know that our work took a toll on our friends and family, too. We walked this earth with starlight in our veins and left behind that awareness in the rocks and the soil, the waters and the air. Even with the ways of regeneration we had learned from the great Druid priests, this process drained us of our life force.

⚜ ⚜ ⚜

I remember a time when we were all together. We were in the place you call France. It was a starlit night, and there we were, sitting around a roaring fire made by the children, with the help of their uncle. Martha had cooked us a delicious meal. Our bellies were full. And the children had collected an enormous pile of dried out wood for the fire.

Yet on that night Yeshua seemed disturbed. In a rare moment of solitude, we took a walk after dinner. I questioned him about his mood, and what he said startled me, for the timing was not to my liking. I pleaded with him to tell me more.

My beloved said a vision came to him earlier in the day—a vision of the Creator Beings that were going to visit us on this Night of

Destiny. We had been visited by them before, as had the teachers who came before us. But the children had not been exposed to this kind of contact. As a mother, I found reasons to turn away from my calling and argue that they were too young to know what was about to be thrust upon them. Already my mind was filled with dread. It was as if I was back in time reliving the trauma of my parents' unexpected passing. And just like that moment, my family would be changed forever.

"Miriam, I did not choose this time. They did," Yeshua responded.

"Can you not talk them out of it? The children are not ready."

"If they are coming to tell us the next stage of our mission, I cannot argue with them. You know that."

"Why can we not live as others? Why have we been forsaken a simple life? Why is our teaching and healing work not enough for them?

"You know the answer to that."

I turned away from the piercing glare of his eyes, for I could not bear the truth that he spoke to me. I knew we were trained for this time, but in this moment, I wanted to take my family and friends and build a fortress below the earth to hide from the Creator Beings. I was tired of being in service to them. Why had I agreed to such things?

Yeshua knew from the depths of his soul that he could not turn away from this cosmic command. I looked back into his eyes and knew our time together was coming to an end. I could feel it in my bones. But before I could speak a word, he pulled me towards him and held me tight. I broke down in tears—the tears that were cried by a woman in love, a woman who was content to teach the locals the teachings of the Way and let time bear witness to their veracity.

Yet this was not to be. I knew that and so did he. But it did not stop my heart from aching, nor did it stop Yeshua from comforting me. He was far less attached to earthly things than was I, and that seemed to make all of this easier for him. Please don't misunderstand me. Yeshua loved his family and treasured our time together. But he had learned so much in faraway lands. He understood the value of detachment in this world—whether that be to riches or to people. He was going to ascend fully in this life, and he was going to become immortal. That had been written in stars since the very beginning, and he never lost sight of that!

⚜ ⚜ ⚜

When we returned home, the fire was shooting tall flames to the night sky. The children were delighted at their handiwork, and immediately sought our approval. Yeshua picked up the child he called—little one from the stars—and swung her around as if he had not a care in the world.

I marveled at his presence, and in truth, it made me love him even more. He was such a strong and caring father, and the children were going to be devastated by his absence. But he was willing to sacrifice everything for the galactic light proliferation to come in our world.

"Father," our oldest began, "is it true that tonight the Blue Beings will come?"

"Who told you that son?"

"I saw them last night, in my sleep. They came to me."

"What did they tell you?"

"They told me they will come here tonight, when the fire was burning bright!"

The other children shrieked with excitement and shouted out many questions. Yeshua took command and explained to everyone that it was indeed true they were traveling from the stars, from their homes far away, to be with us and tell us of wondrous things to come.

This scared our little one and she ran into my outstretched arms. I held her close, for she had already been traumatized by the hardships of moving around as secretly as we did. She did not understand why we were such a hunted people. And no matter how gifted a healer she would later become, she would never fully recover from the separation our family soon would endure.

⚜ ⚜ ⚜

As we sat by the fire, singing the songs of our ancestors, the Blue Beings—the Creator Beings—began to appear and form a circle around us. The children laughed with delight at the phenomenon that was unfolding. Once their circle was complete, a being formed more fully human and moved towards Yeshua. It was such a beautiful blue; its radiance was shimmering.

There was communication between them—gestures and hand movements by Yeshua. He nodded his head in agreement and then asked our son—the one who had dreamed of their arrival—to come forth and stand with him.

My son began to lift up and float; he began to speak aloud words he did not know. As time passed, he was lowered back to the ground and delivered their instructions in a language we could all understand. He spoke of how we were to scatter in the world, each of us traveling to many lands and instructing their inhabitants on the teachings of the Way.

I must stop and ask—were these blue beings from Sirius?

Why do you ask?

I've read in the Wingmkaers material that they and the Atlanteans helped the Annunaki design our human body. They specifically say "The Annunaki had some kind of a falling out with the Atlanteans, and began to conspire with the Sirians and another race referred to as the Serpents. Each of these three races was interested in figuring out how to embody physical planets."

This is a very complicated situation.

They go on to talk about the human programming and that the Sirians were very much the ones who created this programming. They say that the Sirians made the implants for this programming that would be placed inside of us, and that these implants "could propagate through reproduction." There was trickery involved and as a result, the Atlanteans were enslaved by the Annunaki, but with the help of the Sirians. Is any of this true?

This subject is deeply complex because there were so many twists and turns along the way.

The Sirian race did indeed create the programming implants but from a far advanced perspective than this material describes to you. They were not operating from the human experience so their goal was to produce an implant, a seed structure, to see if they could develop the consciousness in human form. From their standpoint, this was mechanical. They did not know there would be such trickery by others. They were trying to animate density more fully. They were hoping this animation would occur so in time, they could express themselves in a different way. You must understand that their form was not the same as ours.

So their operating system was far more advanced than the Atlanteans?

Yes, so far advanced that indeed anomalies were created from these experiences. But at some point the Sirians understood that their implants were malfunctioning, not producing the desire they had hoped for. They needed to make corrections to the human race that was evolving at this time. This is where my beloved Great Mother Isis took on form.

So you're saying that things were going terribly wrong and they needed to fix their mistakes?

Yes, things were a mess, and they had to be fixed.

And that's why Isis was introduced—to bring forth higher ideals to introduce to humanity?

With the passage of time, the Sirians began to understand the deception that had occurred here on earth. Although they were advanced beings, they were childlike in certain ways. They had observed the human population enough to know that something was wrong. And to make things more complicated, something was interfering with their human experiment—and it was the mineral complexity of the earth herself. They had not counted on that variable!

This is where Great Mother Isis enters into creation. When you contemplate this, you will know why my mother nurtured my connection to the earth, and why she insisted I use my powers for the good of my people. Now you see why I was instructed in the ways of the goddess.

That's profound. Does that mean the Sirians introduced Isis to bring forth our connection to the earth?

They did not anticipate the earth interaction with the human body to be as powerful as it was. They did not understand the information and energies stored within the crystal realm could interface with our DNA to restore our memories. This was a unique situation and one that required prolonged observation, since each turn into density produced its own alterations upon humanity.

Is there any evidence of this in our genetic code?

Yes.

Is this what author Gregg Braden means when he says the message in first layer of our DNA has been decoded and translated to mean—God Eternal within the body?

That was part of the rewrite. Now that you see *why* it was necessary, you can understand how Yeshua accepted this part of his mission, even though it would keep him from his family for the remainder of his life.

That's sad. I'm sorry you had to sacrifice that love.

My beloved always said that we were blessed to have the time together that was allotted to us. He reminded me how rare our love truly was.

Were you twin flames? And if so, how is that different than soul mates?

We had moved beyond our karmic ties and into the realm of deep compatibility. Soul mates can be together for a lifetime, but then again, their time together can be very short. Together they have lessons to learn and karmic charge to burn off in their energy field. Soulmates can love each other; they can also be great sickness of the mind in their unions.

When twin flames unite, the union of these two souls can produce tremendous benefits for each other, for their offspring, and also for humanity. They can reach the depths of despair and soar above the clouds, but there is always mutual love between them. They can even achieve a state of love together that is eternal. It is a heightened state of being. And this union has great life force. You are given the chance to merge your souls together in the Realm of Light. This is when twin flames can merge back together as one!

My beloved told me the memories of our time together sustained him in his darkest hours. But he believed we were creating a better world in the coming age. He was right, for although it took much time by human history, it is but an instant in time in the Immortal Place.

The Immortal Place?

I knew you would question that.

Yeshua will answer those questions in great detail for you. You are being prepared to learn of immortality now, and he is the one to teach you of it.

So what did the Blue Beings say to you on that night?

They formed pictures and images so we could see future timelines. They showed us how our cellular nature was changing, even in that moment. They said they were the catalyst for genetic evolution on the planet and that it needed to continue, according to plan. With my understanding of the serpentine energies on earth, they would use me to replicate these waves upon the land in many places, so they could encode the creation stories in the lines of energy, to be remembered by initiates when the time was right. They had details for each of us, according to our abilities.

Did they speak words to you?

No. It was a transferring of knowledge through light and sound waves.

How many different time periods did they show you?

They showed us different world events, and inserts of experience into the program at designated times. This was a way of explaining their long term plan for humanity. They showed us what our part in this transformation would be. You see, we knew then what our future effect would be on many peoples of the earth. Yeshua saw the unfolding of his story, and while he did not like the corruption of his teachings, he did understand why it would happen the way it unfolded. As for me, I loathed what was shown to me in the slandering of my name. But I was also shown the raising of the feminine wisdom, and how it would reveal itself in the future time. That at least allowed me to see right action take place. So our choices were either to reincarnate and progress through the distortion life after life, or to ascend fully and radiate the Creator's light in a different way.

So you and Yeshua chose ascension?

Yes. We had been shown a way to merge our souls together, to blend our light bodies to become one. It was a deeply complex process but Yeshua assured me we could do it. He dedicated himself to mastering that process so we could come together in this way for all eternity.

Did it require you to ascend together?

We were shown how to create the framework for our collective energies, and how we each could flow into it when we had achieved a certain state of being.

Did the children receive the option to do this with you?

No.

Why not?

I asked my beloved this question and this is what he told me. "Miriam, they need to reincarnate back into the population, for that is how their gifts will be expressed. That is what has been decided." And just like that, he was at peace with this understanding. He then added, "They were not given the choices we were given. It is not a punishment but a reflection of their growth at this time."

How could they not be with us in the dimensions of immortality? My beloved spoke again. "Miriam, look at me. These agreements are made in advance of our life on earth, so that the desires of the world do not enter into our decisions. Do you understand that?"

"Of course I do!" I snapped back at him.

"Then why do you act like this?"

"You will never understand how a woman longs for her family to be together. They have such gifts, and we need to help them develop them. This is a great work we have achieved together. Why should it now be torn asunder?"

"It is not."

"Yes it is. We will travel to different parts of the world, and all the while, our hearts will long for each other. How will that help us stand in our mastery?"

"We will have moments to reunite. You saw what they showed us. There will be times we will come together and enjoy each other as we do now."

"Yeshua, it is a savage world! We will be exposed to many dangers. And we will not be together to help each other with our powers."

"Miriam, you are speaking like a frightened child now."

"I am not!"

"You must find your resolve. This is what you and I both agreed to do. It is written in the stars, and there is no way out of it."

"Yes there is!"

"You know the consequences of those actions."

⚜ ⚜ ⚜

There was much drinking of wine after the Blue Beings left us. Even I drank to excess, wanting to drown out the realities that had come so quickly on that night. Thankfully they had given us time to prepare for our journeys, to make proper provisions, and to plan our first reunion.

For me, that was the only ray of hope in an otherwise dismal future. I know this sounds terribly selfish. And I know you think of me as a perfected being. But again I make no apologies for my feelings, for they are what inspired me to complete my work, so when I did unite with my beloved, it would be for eternity. As for my children, their choices were their own and, in time, I would come to accept that.

So please tell me what the rest of your life was like, separated from Yeshua and the children?

What do you think it was like?

I do wish to tell you from where I now exist, everything is complete and I am at peace. But it took many years for me to accept this stage of my earthly life and remain committed to my people.

Where did you go? What did you teach?

I traveled to many places in the world. My home was France, for the wonders of the earth there were like no other place on earth. There was much beauty in that land, and so much magic.

⚜ ⚜ ⚜

There were travels to what you now call Spain and Portugal, and then back to Egypt. Returning there helped me immensely. In time I recaptured my enchantment with High Magic. That is where my daughter learned to become a great healer. She was much like her father in that way and perhaps even more so. She always found herself by someone who was in ill health, and between her training and her understanding of plant magic, she was able to heal many ills.

I taught her and others the wisdom teachings of the Great Mother Isis.

Can you be more specific?

I taught those who were ready to use the earth energies to provide sustenance for their survival. And I taught them how to advance their consciousness by using those same energies.

How did you do that?

I taught them how to identify the strong points of energy on the land. And we spoke incantations as taught to me by the Ancient Ones. These were words of great power. At these special places, we could pull from thin air that which we needed—like edible light.

Edible light?

Manna, the light substance of the visitor beings. And in these places we could drink of the living waters.

Living waters?

Crystalline waters filled with light.

So you were supporting your light body and teaching others how to do that?

Yes, but it required much initiation to do so. The life force in these substances was pure light, and one must be ready to ingest such purity without it making them sick.

Did many succeed in learning this?

More than you might imagine. People were desperate to break free from the harshness of that time. They were eager to learn the secret teachings of the Ancient Ones.

How did this happen?

I followed the initiatory stages of my early training. It was a way of insuring the personal safety of the initiates, and monitoring their spiritual readiness, step by step. These were tried and true methods practiced throughout time.

So you were traveling back and forth to Egypt?

Yes.

Did you ever bring any of your initiates there?

Yes.

How did you make these voyages?

There were many ways to do so. My people were a seafaring people.

Did you work there in secret?

Yes.

Was it necessary for you to do so?

We were always a hunted people.

Who helped you remain anonymous in Egypt?

People from the highest levels of power. They wished to learn the teachings of the Way. They were interested in the Immortality Teachings, and they had lost records from the time of Pharoah Akhenaten and his predecessors.

Why were you all so hunted?

We had mastered very powerful teachings! The Roman Empire considered us their mortal enemies.

Why?

First and foremost, the loyalist Romans were about money and power. They were about excess, greed, and brutality. At their core, their behavior was an extreme expression of mental programming. You could say they were victims to it, even with their worldly accomplishments. And when they became the Holy Roman Catholic Church, the innocent lives they sacrificed in secret were evidence of their enslavement to the predators.

That really sounds creepy.

This is what we were up against for most of our lives. This is what our children were up against, and their children. We did our best to spread the light upon the earth during our time here. That is why Yeshua accepted that our family would be sent in all directions, each of us merging our light bodies with the light body of the earth. He understood that when we were called upon to complete our destiny, there was no negotiation with those who were guiding the evolution of the planet and all sentient beings. He knew what the opposing forces would do if they succeeded with their evil upon the earth, and my beloved was not about to let that happen!

I struggled with our mission because I was more attached to earthly pleasures than he. Some say my time in Egypt kept me more anchored in my body. I was able to do the work for I had been trained to perfection. Yet, in that high ranking of my abilities, I felt like a novice in the presence of my beloved, for I longed to be with him in every moment. My connection to Great Mother Isis kept the feelings of fertility pulsing in my veins. And to be with Yeshua was the most sensual pleasure I had ever experienced. He was more air and I was more earth and water. But together we were fire!

When my beloved left, I knew in my heart it would be a very long time before I would see him again. My sons went with his family to blaze their trails of light in the distant lands of Britain and beyond. My daughter stayed with me. Martha and Lazarus were never far from us, and that gave me great comfort.

My beloved traveled far and wide to blaze the trails of light only he could have done in this world. I truly admired his commitment to humanity. He worked tirelessly to bring the starlight down from the heavens and place it in chosen locations around the world, in places you would never think he walked.

Did he walk in the Americas?

Yes.

Did you?

Yes.

Did you walk the Americas together?

Yes, once.

Can you tell me about this voyage?

It was getting colder in the seasons. We had to make the voyage to return something to the ancient city which had drifted at the time of the flooding of the earth. I was in possession of a treasure from the Great Motherland and it was time to return it to its proper place for safekeeping.

Yeshua said that it would lay dormant for a thousand years or more, but that the Guardians of the Grail would retrieve it one day and keep it safe until the founding of the great city born from the motherland. You know this place now as America.

We performed sacred rituals there. There was a small group of us who traveled there to establish the trail of light in that most beautiful place. We used our knowledge and skill in the blood mysteries to soak our light deep into the earth, so when Yeshua returned at a later time, he could resurrect that light and move it through the land to the western slopes.

Where in the West?

He will tell you when you receive his Immortality Teachings. For now I will tell you that it was his duty to bring the light forth so that in a future time, that light would be recognized by my beloved Knights of the Temple. And the tribal people of America helped us immensely. They were instrumental in protecting the places of light upon the land and keeping the sacred fires burning. Many tribes had contact with Yeshua. They were also visited upon by the Blue Beings, and later, by our valiant knights who encountered more opposing forces than you could ever imagine. But they were strong and powerful men, and the blood of our kin ran through their veins.

Was there a temple underneath the earth here in America?

Yes there was, and it was a stunning temple built in splendor and opulence to the great goddess in her original form.

In her original form?

Long before her presence in the Land of Khem.

What treasure did you have with you?

A stone of great importance!

Can you tell me about this stone?

It was not of this world. To anyone in its presence, it was alive with an intelligence all its own. It could do things that seemed impossible.

Like what?

It could move through time and space. It could disappear and reappear right in front of your eyes. It could calm the winds and part the seas, and it could shoot light through you like a laser beam. It could move about and stop in a flash, all the while sounding the notes of creation.

It could create everything from nothing depending on your desires.

It could also perform surgery to heal a physical body in a very short time. It would burn the affected area and leave a residue. But before you could fathom what just happened, it could clear the area of all traces of surgery and produce a healed and whole body. It was magical and it was mine for a time. We used it in our work, but when we were told it had to be returned for future generations to rediscover, we made the long trip to the lands across the sea, to place it on the emerald altar of the long lost temple.

Is this stone in someone's possession now?

The stone is yet to be found, although many have tried to find it.

Do you know when it will be found?

Its powers are needed in your world.

Can you tell me more?

This stone will call out to those who have worked with it before.

Is it connected to the Ark of the Covenant?

It is part of the phenomenon associated with the Ark of the Covenant.

I've channeled through Ra-Ta that the gold in the Ark of the Covenant was superconductive. Ra-Ta, as Edgar Cayce's Egyptian/Atlantean aspect, said this gold was harvested from meteorites, and it has the thoughts of God within it. Can you elaborate on this, in relation to this stone?

Do you not have the spark of divine intelligence within you?

I will say this. The stone I guarded had the thoughts of the Creator within it. And when this stone was in the presence of the gold on the Ark, both elements entrained to each other.

Then what happened?

That is for you to figure out. Put the pieces together, and observe what happens.

This stone and the Ark?

Yes. But first they must be found!

For now, know that each one of us traveled far and wide to spread the teachings and plant the seeds of light. It would be years before we all would come together again. But when we did, my heart was lifted from its melancholy. After all the years of imbuing the earth locations with starlight, when my family finally reunited, I cried for two days.

Were all of you together?

Yes, and there were more. The boys had married, and had families of their own.

What about your daughter?

She and I were inseparable.

Did she ever have a family of her own?

Yes, she had a daughter. Her husband died, but her daughter was born of pure light.

Did Yeshua meet his granddaughter?

He did. And when he held her, his heart would light up. You could see it through his robe. That is how much love he had for that precious child.

Tell me more about this gathering.

Everyone was there.

What was that moment like when you and Yeshua were reunited?

How do you think it would have been to see the love of your life after not seeing him for all those years? It was overwhelming! But I was grateful to be in his presence once more, to lay with him as husband and wife, to feel his precious body next to mine.

What did you say to each other?

There were no words that could convey our feelings. We held each other tight. He stared into my eyes; I stared into his. We united with an intimacy that defied explanation, for we would never lose that attraction we felt for each other.

⚜ ⚜ ⚜

We feasted for days. And we sat around the crackling fire, each telling stories of what we had encountered along the way, what kinds of people we met, and how we brought the stellar light down unto the land. We talked about what happened inside our bodies every time we did that! Our blood became liquid light. It would make us rise up from the ground and float around!

We danced our sacred dances and whirled the small children round and round, hugging and kissing them constantly. Yeshua told stories like never before.By this time, though, I could see that he had acquired so much light inside of him, that he was beginning to lose some of the edges of his physical form. He had become even more luminous.

He was such a beautiful soul and I held onto him every moment of every day that we were together. Our passion embarrassed the children at times, but we did not hold back, not once.

How much time did you get to spend together—all of you?

We came together for an entire summer. It was glorious. The land was alive with crops and the waters kept us cool in the heat of the day. We were abundantly blessed with all the pleasures of life during this time. It truly was heaven on earth.

I was thrilled to meet my grandchildren and teach them the ways of the goddess. I taught them how to create from the earth and what it meant to be in service to their people. But most of all, I was able to laugh deeply with them. And that laughter healed my heart.

I was able to see my daughter put an end to her anger with her father because of his absence in our lives. I was grateful that she could come to that understanding, for I bore the guilt of how my sadness had influenced her.

She also spent time with her brothers and got a respite from all the healings she performed for her people. Her energy body was restored, and Yeshua taught her new techniques he had learned in his travels.

The two of them and their healing magic was a sight to behold!

I will forever treasure that summer, for it was the last time we were all together.

Did you ever see Yeshua again?

Yes.

The next time we saw each other we began to plan our ascension, for by this time my beloved had acquired even more light. He had learned new ways of merging our light bodies during his time in the East, and he was ready to begin bringing our flames together as one.

Can you explain this process of joining your light bodes together? What was its purpose?

We had decided to merge them so we could become a unified field of consciousness. We could be the sun and the moon, the masculine and the feminine, all polarities reversed and transfigured. The process itself was complex and involved bi-location from one place to another, while we held awareness in both places simultaneously.

It is about creating a stamp of your genetic profile through wave form that is alive and light-filled. It is placed at key locations on the earth. This coincided with the work we were already doing. So once certain geometric configurations were stamped at every nodal point, we could then fill in the empty space with our genetic material. It was like being a great painter.

We used a technique I had learned in my temple training and blended it with Eastern traditions. Even still, we were not certain it would work. But we always believed we would be together for all eternity. So perhaps that belief made it happen.

I've heard from a distinguished teacher in the UK that there are certain places on the earth where the light-bodies of the Masters reside. Is this true?

Yes and no.

In the past there were certain locations where these energetic signatures were kept as a library. Certain books of genetic material were collected at the library and dispersed throughout populations to help them remember certain concepts, ideas, and memories.

But the process is different now.

How so?

This process once had the Great Architect as an overseer. Some call that energy Thoth, Djehuty, Hermes. But truly it is more a vibration than a person. Specific profiles help the human mind of particular cultures. But now there is no librarian overseeing the circulation of energies. That is complete. As you walk through the Eye of the Needle, you are free to move about on our own.

We are finally free to do that?

Yes. How wonderful is this freedom you have been given. I've explained the process of moving through the Eye of the Needle without the ego mind in control. Move in that way and you will create your own destiny in this brand new Age.

Did you achieve your union together in the Immortal Place?

Yeshua sought a way for us to come together and create something spectacular. He loved the excitement and challenges of our union, in all its facets. He was not one to be blocked by the impossible; instead he was one who rose above limitation and created from the love of sacred union. He was a remarkable man, capable of conscious creation in every moment of every day!

It was a perfect way for us to complete our mission, knowing we were creating eternity for ourselves. This is part of the Immortality Teachings. Yeshua will come to you soon enough.

Why now?

It is time to level the playing field. Those are his words. It is time to release this information for those who take these things to heart and follow the pathway of illumination.

Is it in response to something going on in our world, something hidden from us? It is transhumanism?

Yes, and it is hideous. It is a genetic manipulation that cannot continue without dire consequence to many species.

How will the Immortality Teachings help us to deal with this manipulation?

It will balance the artificial intelligence with the natural ways. Yeshua will tell you. And you will understand, for he is a great teacher.

⚜ ⚜ ⚜

You must know that Yeshua and I defied the corrupted powers that be and lived from our mastery. We knew the extent of our abilities for our lives had been dedicated to this purpose. We knew what we could do to place harm in the way of others who sought to destroy us. But the Ancient Ones always reminded us that we were given these abilities to be used for good. If we made a choice to use our powers for wrongdoing, we would be stripped of our divine providence.

I tell you this so that you will understand how we experienced human emotions. We felt conflicts that we had to overcome. We were not pure in every moment of thought and deed, but we quickly learned that purification of thought and deed was the only way to mastery. And if we wanted to master our destiny together, we had to fulfill our destiny for the advancement of humanity. And if we did this together, we would forever be united in spirit. Our energies would never be separated again. We would live in each other's soul for all eternity!

⚜ ⚜ ⚜

You should also know there were many master souls from lands across the globe who shared their most valuable secrets with us. They understood our Mission of Light here on earth. Some had the same mission. Yes we were guided by the Druids and the Ancient Ones, but there were many masters along the way, from all faiths and disciplines who helped us to succeed, for the power of love tears down walls, no matter how high.

Mary Magdalene: Provemce Region, France

Chapter 2
The True Baptism

On my September 2014, trip to southwest France, I stayed at Maison Christina, a charming bed & breakfast situated on the river in Rennes les Bains. This village of secrets is located close to the equally mysterious hilltop village of Rennes le Chateau.

One day while there, I walked down the street to the public garden of Dr. Paul Courrent (1861–1952). He's an interesting figure in the mystery of Rennes le Chateau. He was a contemporary of both Abbe Henri Boudet (of Rennes les Bains) and Abbe Berenger Sauniere (of Rennes le Chateau.) In addition to his duties as a medical doctor, Dr. Courrent was an author, an archaeologist and historian. In short, he was quite an accomplished man.

It is said of the good doctor that he spent time with Sauniere during his last days. Some believe that on his deathbed in 1917, Sauniere told Dr. Courrent the secrets of Rennes le Chateau. Some even claim that Sauniere handed over the legendary parchments to him.

There are trees and park benches in this lovely garden that bears Courrent's name. So I sat down on a bench above the river and listened to the water rushing by. I breathed in the fresh air and let it fill my soul. Then I gazed at the radiant light upon the water and let it take me back in time.

It was in this timeless beauty that I began to feel the spirit of some of the key players in the Rennes le Chateau mysteries. It was amazing how quickly they made their presence known, as if they were waiting for me to arrive. What follows is the information from the channeled sessions down by the river, while the landscape was steeped in the energies of the New Moon and Autumn Equinox.

Gloria:

I can see that Abbe Henri Boudet is here but he's standing in the background. Before he talks, he would like Dr. Courrent to speak.

Dr. Paul Courrent:

The magic in this area is in the river right in front of us—where it flows from and where it flows to. These are important locations in this mystery. If I said the secrets of Mount Bugarach flowed into the secrets of Mount Cardou, would you understand what I am telling you?

Many of the sacred objects that came here had to be stored in places that were hidden in plain sight. It is not because they were in front of you and you did not see them, but rather that you could *not* see them. These objects were removed by the Templars when that became necessary. But the waters and the land remain potent and alive to this day. That is the magic! That is why these objects were brought here in the first place. They would come alive here, and those who guarded them could learn from their activation. It was a startling way to learn!

We too had that opportunity to learn from certain objects because some things were left behind. But becoming the guardians for these artifacts was no small task. It required constant monitoring, and that drove Berenger crazy!

The Templars learned much from observing these sacred objects, and used that knowledge wisely. They funded the building of great cathedrals in this country and elsewhere to give the spiritual pilgrims a chance to awaken their minds. It was an enormous task in a daunting time, but they persisted, and succeeded against great odds. Are you curious who these people were and why they persevered in the face of grave darkness?

As a doctor, it disturbed me greatly to see the unnecessary suffering that was placed upon people when all along, they could be healed from their ailments. At least Rennes les Bains was a haven for those who understood the ancient healing arts. It was here that so many people were helped, that so much healing took place!

Abbe Henri Boudet (priest of Rennes les Bains):

Mary Magdalene was here. Yes, she bathed in these waters and healed in these waters. She and her group of Essenes cured many people of their deeper afflictions in life.

Mary was strong and beautiful. And she left behind secrets of the healing plants. These secrets were passed down to the Cathar population in the region, as they were great believers in Mary Magdalene and her ways!

Mary was seen by the river and was regarded as a holy woman. Many stood in the shadows and just listened to her. It was her voice that made her most powerful. She was able to call down the light from the stars and bring that light into the body of her congregation. That was communion and the real baptism of spirit! That was her fire!

Mary Magdalene:

I come to you as your sister in Spirit. I come to you so you remember the abilities you once had within you. I come to you to tell you that they will now be reborn in you again.

I am excited you have returned to this land. Know that I will provide more soon enough. And one more thing I wish to say—there is a grand influx of light to come upon your planet. This event will help many more hear the call.

Two days later, I walked back to Dr. Courrent's garden, eager to make contact again. It was another warm, sunny day and the river was rushing. That sound alone was music to my ears.

As I settled in and awaited visitation, I noticed the translucence of matter like never before. I could see the light in the water, the light on the water, the light particles in the atmosphere, and the light in all matter around me. Everything was light.

While sitting in Dr. Courrent's garden, I could see Mary Magdalene as she was healing people in this river long ago. Mary was performing healings on the local people, but there were many people who traveled far and wide to receive this baptism, too. I could distinguish them by their clothes and their mannerisms. Some seemed quite cultured and sophisticated; others appeared very simple in their ways.

I saw Mary as she instructed a group of healers surrounding her. They were working as a team. The people in her group knew how to pull the emotional charge through the layers of energy surrounding each person. These imbalances were guided into the waters, and then washed away downstream. I'm not sure how they knew to do this, but they followed her directions with precision. Magdalene said these were Essence teachings, but that they came from the Therapeutae in Egypt.

I watched Magdalene scan the person in front of her. Then she moved in a clockwise elliptical motion, swaying round and round. It felt like she opened a vortex, and by moving this way, she activated the energy field of the matrix. As she scanned the person, she knew where the blocks were, and she began to call out to the life force in a primal language. The life force seemed to understand her commands. It was breathtaking to watch and felt so familiar to me.

These sounds made me wonder about Abbe Boudet's strange book called *The True Celtic Language and the Cromlech of Rennes les Bains*. Could this peculiar book contain references to these hidden words of power?

I watched Mary Magdalene call out these words to an unseen force. She called out again. Then something happened. A holographic six-pointed star formed over the head of the person receiving the baptism. This hologram then moved down into the crown chakra, where it began to spin off into other geometries of light.

Magdalene's group became one with this intelligence as it moved through the energy field. They knew how to grab hold of the imbalances that were spun out in this process and pull them down through the body. I could see it took both spiritual *and* physical strength to do this.

As the distorted energies were corrected and ready to exit through the feet, the person was tipped backward, and the Flower of Life organized. I could see it. It too was holographic in nature. Mary Magdalene's mastery called forth the primal words of creation in order to remove all that was out of harmony with the divine blueprint. And as a sign of success, the Flower of Life formed to show them the baptism had been completed. That was their sign.

Mary also showed me all the people that had come here throughout time to be rejuvenated by the waters and the air and the salt and the soil. She said some stayed on to further learn of the teachings of the Way.

This baptism was an ancient healing technique that cleared the body of distortion. This technique extracted negative emotion that had been trapped in form. The purpose of clearing this charge was to process the unprocessed emotions that were in the person's field of energy. In my Magdalene Circles through the years, Mary always emphasized the importance of clearing the emotional body. She often said when we do that, life force moves about more freely, and the blood carries unimpeded instructions throughout the body to the cells wanting that information. When this happens inside of us, she says our genetic code further unfolds. The lotus flower opens within us and showers us with the infinite expression of love.

This clockwise rotation created a vortex to structure the water inside the human body, thereby making it coherent. In addition, the convergence of the two rivers upstream, the Blanque and the Sals, could very well contain Ormus elements. That means the river that flows through Rennes les Bains is extremely coherent. In this way, this highly intelligent water has incredible healing properties. Once I made those connections between the water in the river and the water inside the human body, Mary was ready to speak.

Mary Magdalene:
The time to deliver the True Baptism is now.

Your world is at a critical point in its spiritual development, and there are many who are lost. Cosmic evolution depends on their evolution, and the evolution of the earth, for there is no separation. Your people must begin to understand such things.

You were once part of these teachings and you were once in the Temples of Light in Egypt. It was there that you learned the balance of earth, the harmony of the heavens, and how we were an expression of both, truly of The All.

There were great moments in the temples—of expansion, of light, of celestial seeding. But with the passage of time you have forgotten these moments. You have forgotten the infinite power to move in and out of form—back and forth—playing, creating, and living your experience with every fiber of your being.

Many of you now find yourselves in a state of extreme contraction. You have been made small and are living in a very controlled world where everything is monitored, where everything is recorded. You do not realize the power the forces of darkness are trying to use against you. I do not wish to dwell upon their evil, but you must realize their reach into your lives.

The healing work you are now doing is crucial to your success! Please continue to forgive yourselves and others for the wrongs of the past. Love yourselves and others with all of your heart, for that is the key to wholeness. Heal your people with elixirs made with special waters. Heal your people with light. You are opening the door to a better understanding of how to use these elements to benefit your restoration.

When your energy field is brought into harmony and reconnected to The All, the pineal gland in your brain center opens fully. It showers the body with an anointing of fluid that wakes up those sleeping cells. You can say that your Book of Life then opens. And what a book it is!

The most strenuous part is to clear the distortion. Once that is accomplished, the opening happens naturally. You give the body the emptiness it needs to activate the flowering of life.

So how does one distill the distortion and transmute it? You must move through your initiations to allow the emotional body to clear, the mind to be set free, and the soul to soar. You must purify your vibration as you go, so you close the gap in your process from where you are to where you want to be. That is the purpose of initiation—to move you from separation to oneness, step by step. And know that when the need to help others becomes great, the doorway opens to this light in a much bigger way, for that level of intensity will be needed in your world. You will know it by the darkness that precedes it, and the solar winds that accompany this earth-shaking time.

Gloria:

After this channeling, Mary Magdalene reminded me that in her time there was much gold in the earth. That gold enhanced the experience of the True Baptism. She said this element will have to be brought back into the process in some way.

There was a lot of gold in Ancient Egypt, and that there was good reason for that. In the past there was gold in the earth in the Rennes les Bains area. That helped her do the work she did there. The gold multiplied the process exponentially and opened the door to longevity in some way.

Furthermore, when Ormus elements are activated, part of that expression vibrates in another dimension. At least that's the current thought. So when that element becomes active within us, we just might be enhancing our dimensional capabilities.

When I've ingested quality Ormus, things appear more transparent, like an Alex Grey painting. I touch upon the translucence of matter, and understand the flow of life throughout the living organism. This might sound crazy but that's the enhancement. That's the upgrade we're entitled to. And it's all within us.

As Ormus furthers the flow of light within us, and when we operate from that light, form begins to break down. If you remember in the second volume of *Mary Magdalene: Revelations From A First Century*

Avatar, when Magdalene sits in the river and has barely a trickle of water to work with, she raises the river flow for the benefit of the villagers (p. 7). In that story, Mary says when she gets going, she transforms from form to non-form. She then begins to create from that frequency.

It's been shown to me this way before, and it goes something like this. The matrix of life is all around you, within you, above and below. It's omnipresent. As you begin to organize creative perception, particles begin to organize around your thoughts. But the brain at play is within the heart chamber. This energy then organizes into a pattern, and your heart-brain begins to interpret that pattern so you can have a particular experience.

The more I wake up to the nature of reality, the more I realize I'm creating my experiences in the now, according to my choices. And what I create reflects my consciousness at any given moment. It shows me where I'm at, like it or not.

As we move through difficult situations, lessons, our soul evolves. In that process we will expose the shadow side of ourselves. How else are we going to understand what's directing our lives in such an unconscious way? At least the beauty of knowing this is that once we get it, we can create from a whole new range of experience. To me that's the shift from the mental restrictions of the Piscean Age to the spiritual freedom of the Aquarian Age.

That's why I love to be in the Languedoc region of southwest France. The life force is concentrated and moves about more freely. So your healing process, both emotionally and physically, can accelerate because of the earth energies that merge with the celestial energies in this landscape temple.

⚜ ⚜ ⚜

Here's a scientific explanation of this phenomenon from an article posted on October 31, 2014 by Tara MacIsaac for the *Epoch Times*. It supports the possibilities suggested by the way Mary Magdalene accessed the consciousness network and performed the True Baptism. MacIsaac features the comments of Jim Elvidge. Elvidge holds a master's degree in electrical engineering from Cornell University. He also holds multiple patents, and has published numerous articles in peer-reviewed journals. (Article link: http://tinyurl.com/p5fl4vy.) In this article he says the following:

> Quantum physicists have shown that matter exists in an indeterminate or oscillating state until an observer fixes it in a particular form. For example, photons can exist in either wave or particle form, but it is the act of observing that determines which form they take; it is human consciousness that drives the change.

It is the act of observing that determines which form matter can take. And human consciousness is the catalyst for that change. So intent is a crucial component. The article continues:

> Only when someone observes something does it become "real." Otherwise, the inside of the pen or the molecular structure of the flower exist as a sort of indeterminate potential. Elvidge compares this to the way subatomic particles seem to fix themselves from an indeterminate or oscillating form into a more stable form upon observation.

As we observe this phenomenon all around us, it becomes real. But what's becoming real? Do we project our thoughts and feelings so we can understand them? Do we observe our beliefs and emotions to see how they play out in our lives? Point is that perception becomes our reality.

> Elvidge doesn't think consciousness originates in the brain. It is, rather, accessed through the brain. The consciousness could exist in something like an Internet network. He said you can call this network, this place of origin, God or the divine if you want, though he doesn't use those words.

So whatever we call this web of life—whether it's God, the Creator, Great Spirit, a higher power, intelligent design—it's all the same energy. And Magdalene knew how to "observe" the energy matrix. She also seems to have mastered the art of intention. That is consistent with her training—that her mastery taught her how to use the True Baptism for the benefit of her people.

Mary Magdalene: Limoux, France

Chapter 3
Final Questions and Answers

This chapter is all about the questions and answers. Some of the questions are mine and others were sent to me. And just to keep things straight, the questions are in italics.

Mary Magdalene's answers are written in regular text.

ABUNDANCE

Why does abundance elude so many of us at this time, especially financial abundance?

You are right that abundance eludes so many of you. It has been that way for a very long time. As the feelings of scarcity and lack in more recent times have spread throughout your world, the global village has reacted. I tell you it is a way that keeps you stuck in your minds, fearing outcomes and creating those realities. Survival mentality does not support the ascension—which is an infinitely abundant state. Survival mentality will keep you separate from your wholeness.

This is an abundant universe. See that and feel it and you will become it.

You make it sound so simple. But how do we do that?

You must step out of the fear that you hold on to so tightly. Let it go! Believe in the replicating patterns of nature, of all things in harmony and wholeness. Feel the perfection. See the sunflowers in the field and know that abundance is a reflection of you. There is no separation between you and the sunflower field. Become the sunflowers; experience their perfection.

No matter what you think, financial abundance is no different. If money is required to support you here on earth, become the money you desire. If you have conflict with money, examine all that blocks you from your wealth. Be honest with yourself, for money is a hot button of distress and identity for so many people. Remain focused, and in time, streams of money will flow to you again. But let me be clear. You cannot access the universal abundance through fear. You must feel the abundance from the deepest places in your heart. Feel the love and experience the expansion. The universal laws will respond to you in kind, for that is the nature of the law.

My beloved Yeshua was a master at creating abundance. He would sit in a meadow in the brightness of day. He would command from the sun all that was his, according to his birthright, his divine right of spiritual abundance. That is the nature of abundance, and it comes from the heart.

He taught people that which they needed was right in front of them, always. But it was their belief in the lack that brought about their scarcity. "Let go of the tricks of the mind and you will remember your fullness," he would tell his people. Many did not believe him, even with the miracles he performed in their presence!

AMERICA

Since you said you traveled to America, what was it like back then?

It was an immense wilderness filled with trees and gushing waters, unique people and sacred practices. It was filled tribal lifestyles that honored the earth. It was an abundant, fertile place. The goddess was always there in that land, receiving the cosmic light for the future time.

And that time is now. It is a time of rebalancing and a return to harmony. And it will come about one way or another, for the planetary ascension depends on it. Whether by grace or by chaos, earth will require this balance, especially in America.

ATLANTIS IN AMERICA

Did you recognize the Atlantean landscape on the East Coast of America?

Yes, and I longed to be there to walk with the goddess in this place.

What do you mean?

Great Mother Isis.

I don't understand.

She is embodied there, although she has been asleep for a very long time. But she is awakening, for it is mandated that she must rise again.

Who did you travel to America with?

My beloved, and others from our inner circle who took the journey with us.

You said earlier that Jesus was here, too.

We had something to return to the great temple there.

What temple?

The one that has existed for thousands of years.

Is it visible?

It is underground, its entrance buried deep within the forestlands.

In Volume II Mary said that it wasn't then time to reveal information on the Atlantean fingerprint in North America. Is it time now to start to receive this information?

You have reached that understanding in your technology and science, so yes, it is.

Yet with that understanding, you have practiced ways that bring about the equal destruction of your world as they did. The reach of that darkness and corruption in your world is everywhere.

Look at New York City and all that surrounding water. Look at the concrete and stone weighing down on that place. Look at the color of the bodies of water all around it. What do you see? You see dead and dirty water everywhere.

What are you doing with your technology? Are you using it for the benefit of your people and the earth? These are the questions that were ignored in the Great Motherland, and that denial brought down a mighty civilization!

There are other places where the Atlantean fingerprint of North America can be seen. Look at the cities of Washington D.C., Baltimore, Philadelphia, and Boston. And there are others that hold that fingerprint—the conflict between advancement and profit, of intelligence and domination.

So I ask you again—what are the fruits of your labor? What are you doing with your advanced understanding? Are you healing people or making them sicker? Are you educating people or making a mockery of their minds? What is your intent? Do you know? Do you care? Do you see enlightenment or cataclysm ahead for your land and your people? What is your vision?

BLOODLINE

Does your bloodline with Jesus continue today by direct descendants? Are there people alive now that were once a part of your direct bloodline but reincarnated into a different family line? Are there both? And if there is a reincarnation line, do you consider that line to still be a part of your physical bloodline?

This is a great question for it will help many!

Our bloodline descendants have always been free to select other soul groups and reincarnate wherever they thought they could best experience the lessons their souls needed at a given moment in time. And yes, all descendants, whether by direct descent or reincarnation in creative ways, are all part of us. There is no separation of memory.

I will go one step further and tell you this. All descendants who held the memory of the Original Time could stave off full ascension and move about as they saw fit, spreading the memory of what you call Christ consciousness on earth. There were many who chose that option, believing that far into the future they would revisit full ascension when their work was completed. Many descendants are with you now, for it was always in the plan of the Ancient Ones.

CAVES

What effect does going deep into the caves have on humans?

Going deep into the caves is going deep into the womb of Great Mother. And when we do this, we can hear her heartbeat. That beating is primal sound and the caves hold that resonance. When we hear it, we remember creation. We can sense and feel many things that formed in the earth, and on the earth, for earth tells her story to us time and again through her heartbeat.

We can breathe more deeply in caves because the interference of those who wish to do us harm cannot enter into these places. That is why we spent so much time teaching in caves—for even then there was obstruction by forces some would call Archons.

As I have said before, when I was a child the Ancient Ones would find me in the caves and teach me their secrets. For this reason, caves always held a special place in my heart.

CLEARING THE PROGRAMMING

Is there another level of clearing that can be done at this time to release old programming, beyond what we already know to do? Can you tell us more?

I tell you that you cannot fathom the depth of the programming that was placed upon you. You experience the story of me and Yeshua and the others, and you think 2000 years was so long ago. But in truth, the programming has been going on for many thousands of years.

When you make sense of the patterns of behavior in your life, you can release the negative emotions that have you stuck in time. The hardships of past lifetimes will melt away, so let them go!

As you call forth Original Memory, ask that the hidden programs that have been running in your mind to finally be transmuted. These are the ones that run so deep, that you may not know they are even there, just like your modern day computers and spyware!

Feel your feelings but release the negativity, the constriction, and birth creativity from within you. Day after day, with discipline and intent, ask for the programming to fall away and it will.

Ask your mind to let go of all limitations that surround the core of your being. Ask for all that holds you back from your fullness to be washed away. Ask for clarity. Ask for the memory of human potential to be reseeded by the benevolent forces that have always wished this for you.

Ask for purification. Ask to be cleared beyond what you can conceive, and trust with all your hearts that if you act in this way, you will be free of the distortion. And if you stand on the earth and do this—in the desert or by the sea, on mountaintops or deep within caves—this connection will accelerate your purification. The earth knows how to assist you in this way.

DIRECT EXPERIENCE WITH MARY MAGDALENE

How can I come to understand your ways more fully? How can I come to have a direct experience with you?

If you desire to understand my ways more fully, I will be there in your awareness to teach you, to guide you. But you must show a willingness to do the inner work of transformation. This will move you closer to a state of unconditional love and forgiveness, both for yourself and others.

If your heart is ready to be stretched wide open, when you call out my name, I will come to you. I will hold the mirror to your life, and reflect those places that need unconditional love and forgiveness. That is the pathway in, for when you call me through forgiveness you let me know you are ready to be in service to others through love, and not through a sense of ego gratification. To be in service is to love and forgive, without judgment.

My ways are the ways of the heart. Although love and forgiveness open the doorway, there is more to be understood about the heart of the goddess. It is an advanced intelligence that you will directly experience. Call out my name and I will come. But be prepared because my ways will challenge you. They will move you beyond your pain and suffering. And if you remain steadfast in your learning, my teachings will assist you in awakening to The All.

FREE WILL

How much free will do we really have?

In truth, we have free will to a point. As we make our choices along the way, we have free will to choose this or that, and then to move on and experience something else. Our choices spring from a combination of our beliefs, karmic attachments, and soul evolution from lifetime to lifetime.

⚜ ⚜ ⚜

When we do the requisite amount of inner work and choose to merge with The All, our will becomes thy will be done—the moment in my beloved's story that you were told happened in the Garden of Gethsemane. In fact, it did not happen that way.

Yeshua always knew that he would fully ascend when the time was right for him to do so. That moment in Gethsemane reflected his acceptance of the politics of the day. It was a difficult moment for him because he had to expose himself to the trial with Claudia Procula's husband, and that would be tricky. And his energy body would be subject to the barbaric ways of the Roman soldiers. But once he agreed to do this, other plans had to be put in action behind the scenes.

He could have fled into the night but he was much smarter than that. He made a choice from free will, and knew that the resulting actions to be taken on his behalf would involve difficult choices by many people in our inner circle. He knew that our lives would be forever changed by this moment in time but he exercised free will in his decision.

I tell you that Yeshua merged with the Creator much later in his life. It was then his free will was over. His will had to become thy will. You cannot merge with those aspects of yourself and have more than one will leading the way. It simply cannot be.

GOLD

I continue to feel drawn to and connected to gold. I feel there is so much more than monetary value there, and even more than the ORMUS. Is there more to understand about it at this time?

You are aware of the conductive properties of gold, but your understanding of this state is limited. When this precious metal moves into the state of superconductivity, it circulates energy through its composition in many dimensions simultaneously.

Using gold in healing, or on relics used in healing rituals, was to correct the flow of energy in all the layers of the human field. Gold can change your thoughts and it can change your range of perception. It is the universal source element that was brought to earth to carry the original Codes of Creation! It was always intended to be a life line from Source Energy to you.

Gold likes to express itself with the solar energies. It is alive and vibrating, especially in its Ormus state. That vibration can awaken your solar self. It can bring vast awareness through its frequency and withstand that transference. Thus the ancients used it to "phone home".

HOLY GRAIL

What is the Holy Grail?

The Holy Grail has been many things to many people throughout time. But the common thread in all of the stories is that the Holy Grail is a life force. It is a certain kind of energy. It transforms, it heals. But it can kill and destroy. It can bring enlightenment or drive someone mad. It can expand you to be as big as the heavens, or shrink you down to the size of an ant.

INNER EARTH

Can you tell us about hollow earth/ the inner earth realms, Agartha— whatever may be important for us to know?

The inner earth is a realm unto itself. It is and always has been part of your planetary design. Know that there are vast worlds inside the earth, as there are within you. The mystics have always said this throughout time. Discover your inner self more fully, and you will understand the inner earth more fully. Your bloodstream, your bones, your organs, and all the information systems inside of you keep you running smoothly. And so it is with the inner earth.

JESUS AND THE CORRUPTION OF HIS TEACHINGS

What is the most misrepresented part of the teachings of Jesus?

The most misrepresented part of my beloved's teachings is that they were religious. They were never intended to be so. His teachings were altered to create a religion.

Yeshua was not looking for religion, but revelation—revelation through initiation and a deeper understanding of the Mysteries, of the nature of our reality. He came to help people break free of their limitations because of the constructs of mental programming. He never ever wanted his people to be restricted by a religion of false beliefs!

MONEY

Why does it appear that so many people trying to lead authentic lives and seek the truth are having so many financial struggles at this time? Why is this and why does there seem to be no relief in sight?

Money is and always has been far more than just the currency of the day. It allows for the control of people, places and things. So ask yourselves—do you feel controlled by the lack of money in your lives? If so, therein resides your answer.

Your world is deeply attached to materialism, perhaps now more than ever. There is a tremendous surge in the inequality of wealth. So until the great divide is reconciled, you who choose alternate ways of living and expressing yourselves will continue to struggle with money *if* you allow *the beliefs* of those in power to control your thoughts and feelings. If you live in their world and not your own when it comes to money, you give your personal power to everything that is outside of you. But if you stay focused on the feelings of abundance with all your heart, then abundance must come your way. That is the law.

Those of you experiencing this reality must move your awareness from a survival mentality to prosperity. You must shift your awareness and know that the authenticity you seek is the doorway to discovering the energy of money.

Embrace your authenticity rather than being shamed by it! Speak your truth and make no apologies for it. And stay centered in love. When you do this, you will begin to flourish again.

MOST IMPORTANT THING

What is the most important thing we need to know that can help us and others?

Love; when you love someone in the way of agape, you allow them to melt away lifetimes of the pain and suffering they have stored deep inside them. Love them so they can remember love.

MYSTERY SCHOOL TEACHING

Is there is one mystery school teaching that is of the utmost importance right now for us to learn?

It is the teaching of the nature of our reality. When you accept the truth that the stars, the sun and moon, and the salts of the ocean are inside of each and every one of you, then you will remember that the Creator designed everything in its likeness. Nothing can live in a state of separation here on earth. When you bring that understanding into your heart, you will begin to live from that wisdom. Let that wisdom inspire you to become the wholeness of expression that is your divine birthright. That will heal you, the earth, and even the universe.

PURIFICATION

How can we best prepare for the changes that are coming?

These changes you speak of are already here!

The best thing you can do to prepare yourself is to understand the stranglehold of the ego upon your lives. I have said this many times and I will say it again—the ego mind is the illusion that causes much suffering here on earth. But the heart is the compass that will give you necessary direction for your life. Live from the heart and you will be prepared, for the heart will navigate the chaos of change.

ROSES

What can you tell us about the rose?

As the petals of the rosebud open her center, the goddess draws you into her womb. It is the center of the creative force. If you surrender to this force, the rose will releases its fragrant elixir and connect you to the galactic mind.

SECOND COMING

How can we all help raise earth's consciousness both on a daily basis and long term?

If you spend time in meditation as a way of daily discipline, you will cleanse your thoughts from the ego mind and elevate them to receive from fields of coherence. From that state of being, you can experience feelings of wellness, and of original remembrance. Those feelings nurture the collective thought-stream and elevate your world. This was surely an Essene belief. Practiced daily, it will produce long-term results.

How does the collective consciousness determine how soon this will make a noticeable impact?

The impact is already rippling throughout space and time. Many dimensions already feel the impact of the love. These unseen realms already feel the compassion and intelligence of those who wish to enter the new age free from the distortion of many millennia.

Will Jesus appear as indicated in the Bible as a second coming or will it just be his energy that makes an impact on our change? If so, are we coming close to this event?

My beloved will not appear as a person for the Second Coming. That is a non event. That is a misinterpretation of this cycle in time. What is real is the consciousness that he left behind while embodied here on earth. When his ascension was complete, that process created an enormous over-soul in the heavens. And more and more people now resonate with his over-soul. That is the second coming. It is already happening.

STAR KNOWLEDGE

How can we connect with the stars to learn about the star knowledge?

As I have said before, you can sing to them. There is no separation between you and the stars. They are you and you are them. You are resonant frequencies.

Sing to them in the sky at night. Sing simple melodies of your love for them, for their light, and for the portals they create in the sky and within you. Know that you are constantly streaming this knowledge into your cells.

Many people are affected by the cycles of the moon and sun but they do not acknowledge that connection. When the stars align in certain patterns and symbols, they are sending messages. Some say such things are foolish, but I tell you they have forgotten the Star Knowledge. They have forgotten that the stars call out to you each night, as the sun does each day. They stream forth intelligence and energy to your world, and when you thank them for that, they smile upon you.

So make it a regular practice to observe the movements of the stars and receive their messages. Spend time outdoors and connect with the natural elements. Allow the star knowledge to flow through you. Feel the harmony in the Music of the Spheres.

THE MYSTICAL CHRIST

Many have always felt very connected to the mystical Christ. They see him in their third eye. What does this mean? Why does this happen?

It is that over-soul consciousness that is imbued into the universal matrix of thought. When one ascends completely and becomes All That Is, those frequencies can be accessed by all that seek to reactivate their third eye, the pineal gland. That gland is the one that is receptive to the mystical Christ. It is a gateway for that experience.

VENUS

Can you explain how Venus imprints the land in the Rennes le Chateau area of France?

In that place there are streams of light than run through the land. You have felt them there yourself, but you did not comprehend the specifics. Yes, it is the telluric energy there that pulls down the light from Venus. The telluric force then disperses that light throughout the lands. And the result is called heaven on earth.

Heaven on earth refers to a place on the land that interacts with the light of celestial bodies. That interaction creates sounds. Yet these sounds are barely audible, even with a trained ear. But they are there as a living and breathing presence.

I spoke the primal words of the forgotten language and used the telluric energy to command the celestial sounds from on high, into my being, for the benefit of my people. And yes, Venus has always been an integral force in the union of heaven on earth. Remember her transit!

Mary Magdalene: St. Baume, France

Chapter 4
Stars Above, Stars Below

In her bestselling book—*The Camino: A Journey Of The Spirit*, Shirley MacLaine chronicled her pilgrimage as she set out on the road to Compostela. An Amazon review has this to say of her book:

> Known as the Camino, the Santiago de Compostela Camino is a famous pilgrimage that has been undertaken by people for centuries across northern Spain. It is said that this 500-mile path lies directly under the Milky Way and that it reflects the energy of the star systems above it. Facing her sixth decade of life on earth, writer and actor Shirley MacLaine decided to go on this trek. She wasn't sure why, she only knew that the Camino had been traveled for thousands of years by "saints, sinners, generals, misfits, kings and queens. It is done by the intent to find one's deepest spiritual meaning and resolutions regarding conflicts in Self. (Link: http://tinyurl.com/lwh6yqv)

So what does this reveal to us about pilgrimage? First of all, the connection between the Camino and the Milky Way is notable. Here again we have a connection of the stars above and below, something that Magdalene has spoken of time after time. It's suggested that the Camino is a pathway that holds the energy of the star systems above it. Could this be another heaven on earth location, where the stellar energy flows down from above, where the Hermetic principle of As Above, So Below, is fully in play?

We've seen this union of energies before in the Rennes le Chateau region of France. There are also other locations worldwide where this phenomenon occurs. So when I notice the imprint of the stars in these places, it excites me. And when I can connect the stars to the pilgrimage paths of old, it excites me even more.

There are many reasons for people set out on a pilgrimage to far and distant lands. Often pilgrimage comes at a time when our lives lack the luster to sustain us. Perhaps it's something deeper we crave to know about ourselves, our world, or the nature of our reality. Maybe it's a personal crisis that propels us—a divorce, the death of someone in our lives, an illness, or just a need to shift our experience into something more meaningful. Perhaps it's a calling that would eventually trigger us to question our god, our connection to the universe. Whatever drives us to set out on pilgrimage, there's one thing we can say for sure. Human beings have been trekking to sacred sites worldwide for a very long time. In these journeys we seek solace and healing, answers and enlightenment.

⚜ ⚜ ⚜

One of the best known places of pilgrimage is that of Glastonbury, England, UK. In the legendary place of Avalon the great stories of King Arthur and his Knights of the Round Table have captured our imaginations. We know of Merlin and Arthur and the sword being drawn from the stone. We are learning of legends that Jesus and his uncle Joseph of Arimathea entered into this mythical landscape through Cornwall and eventually made their way to Glastonbury. It is said of Joseph that he was a wealthy merchant trading for tin with the ancient miners of Britain.

There are whispers of the grandmother of Jesus called Anna being in these lands. And UK author Graham Phillips suggests that Mother Mary could be buried in Wales, another enigmatic location which holds some very interesting secrets. The author asks if this location holds the real tomb of Mother Mary. And if so, he wonders if this is the location that Giovanni Benedetti, the Vatican archaeologist, was told to keep secret?

⚜ ⚜ ⚜

Glastonbury is the home of timeless legends and grail mysteries. But there's an even deeper connection, one that returns us to the recent revelations of Mary Magdalene.

In their book *The Star Temple of Avalon—Glastonbury's Ancient Observatory Revealed*, authors Nicholas Mann and Philippa Glasson conclude the following:

> ...the alignment to the galactic core may describe an intensification of the cosmic process of transformation, rebirth and renewal... (The Temple Publications, 2007, p. 112)

⚜ ⚜ ⚜

They further suggest that the beliefs of the Maya, the Egyptians and the ancient Britons saw the 2012 Winter Solstice and:

> ...every Winter Solstice of this time...a moment to renew our covenant with Spirit; to make a pledge that not only upholds the balance between ourselves and all of life, but also affirms a truly ancient alliance—the alliance between humans and the stars. (Ibid., p. 112)

⚜ ⚜ ⚜

We have a new body of knowledge about our connection to the stars. Mary Magdalene has revealed it to us with details like never before! And there's support for our connection to the stars in other traditions and practice of ancient peoples. It was believed by these cultures that during these auspicious moments in time, we could expand our awareness to include the understanding of the cosmos, and ultimately of ourselves.

To me, that is a strong motivation for pilgrimage, whether it takes place in far and distant lands, or in the comfort of our own homes. The bottom line is the deep desire to awaken to our truth, and the nature of our reality. And along the way, if we can reconcile our conflicts, square away our disagreements, forgive those who have wronged us, and live from our hearts, we will have achieved a remarkable feat.

Mary Magdalene:
Rennes le Chateau, France

Chapter 5
In the Moonlight

If you find you aren't able to travel to places of pilgrimage at this time in your life, for whatever reason, what follows is a guided journey I created for you to take from your home.

So set aside some time for this voyage of the soul, and create the ambience that suits you. Whether you keep it simple with a burning candle and a warm blanket to cover you, or create something more elaborate like a ceremonial altar, give yourself the time and space to support your journey inward. Lock the door to your sanctuary, turn off your phone, and commit to the journey. Allow yourself the freedom to see what you need to see. Feel what is necessary to restore value to your life. Are you ready to set out on your journey?

Here we go…

Get comfortable in your space. Prepare your altar with what calls out to you—a sprig of sage, your favorite crystal, and image of your guardian angel. Labradorite and rose quartz work well for this journey. Perhaps you're drawn to stones of protection like obsidian. This stone can also provide clarity and dissolve emotional trauma. It can increase confidence along the way.

So light the candle before you and gaze into the flame. Let its light still your awareness deep within you. Then close your eyes. Take a few deep breaths. Call forth your imagination. This is your time, and it is deeply personal. This is your pilgrimage.

THE JOURNEY HOME

You find yourself walking along a dirt road. You're by yourself but you're not afraid. You're on a mission that you've been waiting to fulfill. This mission has come to you in dreams before, but now it's unfolding in your waking reality, thus you finally agree its time has come. You're ready.

It's dark outside but you sense the sun will rise soon enough. In the meantime there is something you must find. It's a long lost fragment from an ancient text. You're not certain which time period it belongs to, but the memory of its existence is deep within you. It has crossed your path before. You feel it in your bones. And you feel the darkness of the night will sharpen your senses and help you find it.

Stop. Listen. What do you hear? Are there sounds of animals in the distance? Can you hear any water flowing across the land? Look up at the night sky and notice the stars above you. Do you recognize the constellations? See any shooting stars whiz by? Will you ask the stars to guide you with their magic on this night, and give you signs when you need them?

Return your gaze to the ground and observe what is before you. Don't let the darkness distract you from your mission. Yes there are forces that want to derail your efforts on this path. But you will persist and you will prevail.

As you walk further down this path, you can feel several small stones beneath your feet. Pick one up and rub it. How does it feel? Does it seem alive to you? Does it have a message for you?

Is there anything in the brush that you can smell—like lavender or sage or something else? Are there flowers or herbs that you recognize growing in this place?

Something calls out in the distance that stops you in your tracks. Could it be the cries of the coyote? Could it be the lament of its prey? Could it just be your imagination?

Stand tall. You're on a mission and you will not be deterred, no matter what the animal medicine is telling you. Pilgrimage is not a straight path but rather a winding road. You remind yourself that you will move forward no matter what your fears are stirring up within you. It's time to break free from all that holds you back.

You walk along your way until you catch the sight of a shooting star above you. You get shivers up and down your spine. You know, by the way that you feel, that you must follow the bend in the road. You must change course and make your way deeper into the woods.

There you walk on, guided by another shooting star. This is your turning point. This is the turn in the road that leads you into the depth of your soul. You take the risk because you must.

Each step takes you deeper into the woods but somehow you are unafraid of the unknown. A welcome trust washes over you. You can hear the stream that was once in the distance getting closer now. You can smell the freshness of the water and feel it opening your lungs. Take a deep breath, and then one more. Make your way closer to the stream. Find a tree stump, or whatever is available to you, and rest for a few minutes. But don't be tempted to drink of this water. It contains a powerful potion that will put you to sleep. You must maintain your senses to their fullest acuity, and remain as focused as ever. There is something beyond the stream, and you must find it.

Take a moment and reflect on those thoughts and feelings that emerge from the cool air of the night. Know that you are being guided by a force that knows exactly where you need to go.

As you move on, you find your way across a makeshift wooden bridge, and cross the stream deeper into the woods. For awhile, you lose your sense of direction. You feel uneasy and a little shaky. So you stop again and take another deep breath, centering yourself to the earth, and the power in this place. You ask the night fairies to lead you out into the clearing, where you are certain is your treasure. And you wait for them to arrive.

They hear your call and come to join you. They show themselves as tiny bright lights in the darkness. They take you by the hand, and walk you forward. They have come because you called them, so trust them to guide you. The night fairies make delicate noises and whish by your face. But they remind you not to underestimate their strength. They know these woods well, and all the forces within them. And they will use their fairy magic to guide you on your path.

You walk along with them and hear your heart beat like never before. Are the night fairies lighting you up inside? Are you getting closer to your treasure? What is your heart telling you?

With the help of your fairy friends, you finally arrive at the clearing beyond the trees. It is a large and spacious clearing. You can once again see the night sky in all its glory. And then, more shooting stars stream past you. The moon is luminous and vibrant. You notice its light like never before. You wonder if it was always this bright but you just didn't take the time to notice it before. Or is everything just more alive in this place?

The fairies point you in a direction of a tall standing stone in the far corner of this field, and motion you to move towards it. You obey their command as you watch them fly away.

As you walk towards this large standing stone, you notice a carving of swirls in its center. It's a simple etching but you know it carries great importance. It has significance for you and your memories from another place and time. Does that lifetime flash before you? Can you see the details?

You are ready to place your hand upon the stone. You are ready to receive its knowledge. You are clear-minded and wish to hear its message for you. This is your moment. This is your journey. Take your time and make sure you are centered in your heart.

And then it happens! The carving in the stone lifts off the surface. It floats right in front of you then bobs up and down. It's reading you like a book. It knows why you're here. And it's glad you have made it to this place. You traversed the unknown and now you have arrived at the true Stone of Destiny.

You watch this spiral move all around you, continuing to scan you from the inside out. It has an intelligence that you don't understand, yet its magnificence renews you sense of wonder.

Time passes. You are nearing the end of your journey. But you sense there is something yet to happen, to complete this pilgrimage of yours. You raise your arms to the night sky and remember to sing to the stars. You shout out your love for their light, and for all the messages they give you every night. You drink from the heavens all that it pours forth. It is the dawning of the Age of Aquarius, and you are drinking from the grail cup of celestial forces while you stand upon the earth. You have found your heavenly place. It is home.

As you turn away from the stone, you sense the sunrise is approaching. It's time to begin the journey back. But then you hear the voice of a woman call out your name. She steps from behind the stone, cloaked from head to toe. You are startled but enthralled by her presence.

She is the veiled one. She is Mary Magdalene.

She walks closer to you with an outstretched arm and places her luminous hand on your heart. She feels your soul as if it was her own. You are humbled by her presence and kneel down before her. Mary then places both her hands upon your shoulders and calls out the words of creation upon you. You look up and watch the stars rearrange themselves in the night sky. They form a chalice and it tips toward you. It's the grail cup. A glowing gold chalice then appears in the hands of the Magdalene and she asks you—will you drink from this cup?

Take a moment and let the mystery of what she offers you settle into your soul. Are you ready to receive her in all her glory? Do you need more time to understand what's unfolding? Whatever your thoughts or feelings might be, honor them. Take your time.

You are ready now, and you wish to drink from the cup. You remember that's why you embarked on this journey in the first place. This is your mission—to know this eternal light, to become it, and to shine the light of the Holy Grail brightly from this day forward.

⚜ ⚜ ⚜

As Mary Magdalene's presence fades away, the moonlight wanes. You call out her name and thank her for what she has gifted you on this night. At the true Stone of Destiny, you have received the light from the stars. Breathe deeply and let this transmission to settle into your bones.

⚜ ⚜ ⚜

Now it's time for you to return from your journey. As you prepare yourself to do so, you hear the faint sound of something behind you. You turn to look and notice a small scroll on the ground. You walk over to it and pick it up. The paper smells musty. You know it's old.

It has written upon it the Secrets of the Ages. You have longed to reclaim this parchment and rediscover its secrets. And in the right time, you will be guided to read it.

You trust this message with your heart and soul. So you pick up the scroll and tuck in under your arm. You know you'll bring it back with you and never lose it again. It is with you now for all the days of your life.

You begin the long trip back, forever changed by what happened on this moonlit night. You realize now that you gathered the courage to take this journey of a lifetime, and you succeeded.

You are relieved, you are at peace. You rejoice!

You have fulfilled your sacred mission.

Acknowledgments

I would like to thank everyone for their incredible interest in the first two volumes of *Mary Magdalene: Revelations From A First Century Avatar*. Thanks to those who were so interested in learning more, that a trilogy was born in the process.

Many thanks to Matthew Giorgio for designing another beautiful cover.

Thanks to Brian Kannard at Grave Distractions Publications for publishing another title, and for continuing to support my work.

Thanks to all the ladies from The Magdalene Circles throughout the United States. Your enthusiasm is my inspiration!

Thanks for those who asked questions, including Kim Bacik, Rene Barnett, Judy Coppi, Karen Heck, Arika Kane, Nancy Loring, Jessica Arael Marrocco, June Petillo, and Betsy Ritchie.

Thanks to all of you who have written to share your insights with me since the publication of these three little books. Again I use the word "little" with hesitation because you've told me that the size was just right. Mary's words were packed with energy so, in this case, less is more.

And for those of you who feel these alchemical effects as you turn the pages and reflect upon the words of Mary Magdalene, thank you for opening your hearts to her inspiring presence.

⚜ ⚜ ⚜

I'm honored to have walked in her footsteps of Mary Magdalene for all these years. Her aura was the mystery of the sacred feminine I so desperately needed in my overly masculine world. I will be forever grateful for the balance her presence has given me. That presence appeared in so many ways in my life, and became my inspiration to complete the Great Work.

About the Author

Gloria Amendola is an intuitive who has a passion for esoteric knowledge and dream language. In her private circles, she blends the western tradition of research and evidence with the eastern path of meditation and going within for answers. She is a trained facilitator and accomplished shamanic drummer, and works with a variety of disciplines in her teaching.

Her travels bring her to sacred sites worldwide to experience these powerful landscape temples firsthand. A modern day Templar aligned to Rennes le Chateau, France, she follows in the footsteps of the enigmatic Knights Templar, walking where they walked, gathering impressions from the traces they left behind.

Mary Magdalene: Revelations From A First Century Avatar, Volumes I, II, and III are the author's first hybrid non-fiction/channeled books. Other titles include her two novels in the *Tower* series. They are *The Tower and the Dream—Awakening to the Call* and *The Tower and the Land—Awakening to the Light*. The author is currently working on the third novel in the Tower series, *The Tower and the Well—Awakening to the Grail*. You can read more about her at www.gloria-amendola.com.

Printed in Great Britain
by Amazon.co.uk, Ltd.,
Marston Gate.